How to Bless the New Moon

the New Moon

The Priestess Paths Cycle
and
Other Poems for Queens

Rachel Kann

Ben Yehuda Press
Teaneck, New Jersey

Published by Ben Yehuda Press
122 Ayers Court #1B
Teaneck, NJ 07666
http://www.BenYehudaPress.com

To subscribe to our monthly book club and support independent Jewish publishing, visit https://www.patreon.com/BenYehudaPress

Jewish Poetry Project #11　　　　　　　　**http://jpoetry.us**

ISBN13 978-1-934730-87-4

cover art by Jessica Tamar Deutsch

Library of Congress Cataloging-in-Publication Data

Names: Kann, Rachel, author.
Title: How to bless the new moon : the priestess paths cycle and other poems for queens / Rachel Kann.
Description: Teaneck, New Jersey : Ben Yehuda Press, [2019] | Summary:
　"Jewish poems reflecting the philosophy of the Hebrew Priestess movement"-- Provided by publisher.
Identifiers: LCCN 2019028839 | ISBN 9781934730874 (paperback)
Classification: LCC PS3611.A54938 A6 2019 | DDC 811/.6--dc23
LC record available at https://lccn.loc.gov/2019028839

These poems were previously published by *Hevria*, with thanks.
The following poems were previously published, with thanks, by:

Mermaid Esther: An Astonishing Fire	*Incandescent Mind*
את	*Eht/Aht (את): a Netivot Oracle Guide*
All of this Outrageous Beauty	*A Poet's Siddur*
Haneshama Lakh	*Tiferet Literary Journal*
Daiyenu	*A Poets' Haggadah*
The Beginning	*A Poet's Siddur*

0 21 / 10 9 8 7 6 5　　　　　　　20200412

Contents

Other Queens

Foreword by
Rabbi Jill Hammer, PhD

Rachel Kann is here to put the ecstasy back in prophecy.
Kann's poems send chills up the spine with their uncanny
beauty and their thirst to name what is true and intricate,
lovely and terrifying. Her use of words is a joy and an
awakening to the sacred within. The body of poems
contained in this volume are multi-genre: liturgy, protest,
love song and affirmation. These poems evoke female
ancestors with gifts that resonate in the present, and they
also summon us, whoever we may be, to actively enter our
own landscapes.

In "The Priestess Paths Cycle," Kann delves into the
thirteen archetypes of the priestess as defined by the
Kohenet Hebrew Priestess Institute: paths of sacred
practice derived from the Bible and Jewish history. (Rav
Kohenet Taya Mâ Shere and I elaborate on them in our
book *The Hebrew Priestess: Ancient and New Visions of
Jewish Women's Spiritual Leadership*.) Kann uses these
thirteen faces as jumping-off points for her explorations
of magical women: women who prophesy, women who
seek, women who dance. "Tell them you've come to
get your drum back," the Prophetess howls. "I hunger
beyond longing," swoons the Lover. "I choose to be made
doorway," whispers the Templekeeper. The Shamaness
says: "Every magnolia has secrets to sing to you." The
Weaver demands: "You must feel the weight of the world,"
and the Wise Woman proclaims: "Your guts have always
known the rhythm." The Fool replies: "You know nothing."
Kann opens the thirteen archetypes up to us with lush and
delicious language that is at the same time challenging and
revolutionary. These varied faces of the holy, of the human,
invite us into our most deeply lived selves. The intertext

of the multiple poems invites us to wonder: who are we? What facets of the universe hide within us?

In "Other Poems for Queens," Kann continues her channeling of ancestral voices. She meets the matriarchs of the Bible, spinning rich encounters from biblical texts, kabbalistic lore, and fairy tales. We meet Esther as a suffering and transforming mermaid, a "lighthouse of a little girl." We meet Rachel the matriarch, a shapeshifter, trickster and wrestler who shapes vessels to receive divine reality. Eve offers: "I did listen to the serpent." The prophetess Deborah reminds us: "Everything flows like honey, eventually." In Kann's vision, the women of the Bible are aware of the cosmos that shapes them, a cosmos they ride like a fairy mount through their own lives. These biblical matriarchs seem to swim through the past, inviting us to discover a certain fluidity in the present.

In "Other Poems," Kann muses on the nature of reality and confronts the paradox of our times. In "Exile and Redemption," she writes: "If it seems like everything's shattering, that's because it is." Yet in "The Higgs Field: Each Green Unfurling, Kann writes: "The miraculous machinery/of your is-ness/if you could witness it/would knock you to your knees in awe…" Both of these things are true—the gratitude and the shattering—and Kann's mission is to help us integrate that knowing into our hearts, minds, and bodies. The core intent of these poems is to invite readers to "rededicate the sacred space at the center of us."

The reverent ecstasy of Kann's poems is not a flight from the real but a descent into it. There is much about the body here, a body not divorced from spirit but rather ignited by spirit. And there is much about the call to speak truth—personal and societal—into a world that tries to avoid it. The poems grasp at liberation, seeking to break through old paradigms, not with rage but with wonder. The deity incarnated in these lines of poetry is not a supporter of the

Rachel Kann

status quo but a power that breaks through convention to seize the heart. In "Illumined Nation/The Rededication of Space," Kann writes: "Grab hold of the narrative, revolt against the same old story." These poems, while they contain strands of ancient tales, have grabbed hold of the prevailing spiritual narrative and shifted it into a new, feminine/feminist circle-dance that brings change and aliveness to the old myths.

To read Rachel Kann's poems is to be confronted with the possibility that you, too, are prophet and beloved, touched by forces far beyond your mundane knowing. So, dear reader, enter into the "perfumed forcefield" of these words— they are healing and transformative. You, like the Maiden Kann celebrates, are the "very mystery we are discussing."

Rabbi Jill Hammer, PhD, is the co-founder of the Kohenet Hebrew Priestess Institute and the Director of Spiritual Education at the Academy for Jewish Religion. She is the author of a number of books, including The Jewish Book of Days: A Companion for all Seasons, The Omer Calendar of Biblical Women, The Book of Earth and Other Mysteries, *and co-author of* The Hebrew Priestess: Ancient and New Visions of Jewish Women's Spiritual Leadership *and* Siddur HaKohanot: A Hebrew Priestess Prayerbook. *She lives in New York City with her wife and daughter.*

Foreword by Rav Kohenet Taya Mâ Shere

How to Bless the New Moon is an offering of exquisite devotion. It is a lovesong to the netivot, the thirteen priestess pathways of the Kohenet Hebrew Priestess Institute, a movement reclaiming and innovating embodied, earth-honoring Jewish feminist spiritual leadership. These netivot can be understood as archetypes for Jewish priestessing, but calling them archetypes is tame. The pathways we work with are ways of women who existed. We know because we uncover their remnants in the Hebrew bible, as well as in earlier texts from the Ancient Near East & later texts from Jewish tradition. We know because they appear in our sleeping and waking dreams and in pulsing remembering in our bones. We know because we yearn for them, because we need them, because we are them. The glowing incantations in *How to Bless the New Moon* bring the netivot to life, transforming these women and these ways from ones who once were, to ones who are—blessing us, beckoning us, railing with us, shining through us—right here right now.

Sometimes, if we listen clearly enough, words shimmer. Sometimes, if we let enough potent possibility drip into our silence, or the spaces between our breath, worlds open and dreams become born. *How to Bless the New Moon* is prayer like that, glistening everywhere. It is deep roots kissing vast vision. It is succulence married to precision. It is gasp after gentle gasp of sweet recognition. With prophecy that masquerades as poetry, Rachel Kann gives voice to the ancient future ones. With a simultaneous fierce call and glowing caress, she incites their flow.

In this luminous volume, Rachel Kann—may her creations, her voice, her vision be blessed—gives us serious, succulent verbal medicine. She doses us with the cosmic blueprints we need to not only imagine that these women once were, she breathes stardust into them so they become here now. So we perceive them—in ourselves and in each other—here now.

Rav Kohenet Taya Mâ Shere is the co-founder of the Kohenet Hebrew Priestess Institute and of Makam Shekhina and is Visiting Assistant Professor of the Practice of Organic Multireligious Ritual at Starr-King School for the Ministry. She has recorded Wild Earth Shebrew, Halleluyah All Night, Torah Tantrika *and* This Bliss *and is the co-author of* The Hebrew Priestess: Ancient and New Visions of Jewish Women's Spiritual Leadership *and* Siddur HaKohanot: A Hebrew Priestess Prayerbook.

How to Bless the New Moon

Rachel Kann

How to Bless the New Moon

Back before the journey began,
before traversing
the massive desert expanse,
before the sea had even split,

way, way back in Egypt,
the first collective gift-transmission
was given:

With transcendental gentleness, the
Indwelling/Ever-Presence/
All-That-Is/Infinite
lifted your chin;
directed your attention
toward the heavens,
said,

Let the moon's cyclic and fluid beauty
hew you to the rhythm
of time's unending spiral,
use this precise present
as your very beginning.

Sanctify every recursive moment of holiness
over objects.
Follow the mystery hidden in shadow.

Seek beneath the surface.

Let others bask in the surety of sunlight.
You were born of the moonlight tribe.

Let others be about answers.
You be about questions.

Live in the liminal.

Listen for the subtle metal-scrape:

these are keys unlocking each restraint.

Listen for the whisper:

this is the giving over
of the calling forth
of the new moon
to you.

Listen, for
this is your liberation.

Rachel Kann

The Kohenet Netivot Sidrah

Neviah / Prophetess

Don't misapprehend
history's dismissal
to be a legitimate reflection
of your alleged invalidity.

This suppression is systemic,
intended to implant you
with self-doubt
and worse.

Tell them you've come
to get your drum back.

They've rehearsed this
for centuries.

They shamed you for your
revelations as a child,
been training you to doubt
your intuition
since the beginning.

It's a matter of tuning in
to the right frequency,
cleaning your receiver,
respecting the sensitivity
of your equipment.

Tell them you've come
to get your drum back.

It's a matter of the gratitude
that knocks you to your knees,
the bravery that looks demons
in the mirror
in the face,
the real sacrifice—
the blood and guts kind—

every destiny
exacts its own heavy price
until you are nothing
but dying.

It's a matter of acknowledging
the well sprung up and
wandering with you
through the wilderness
like a faithful familiar,
mandrake and fennel-flower
issuing forth from the earth
in a ground-corona around it.

It's a matter of quieting,
of listening to everything
until you are still enough to
let the bush of jasmine croon
its swoon perfume all over you.

It's a matter of knowing
you don't deserve it.

Could you have been made
any other way?

Creature that you are?

Have you not prayed and prayed
to be made vessel?

Then be
(not surprised,
but still) amazed
when fluid revelations
channel through you;
are granted safe passage.

You remember, it is a rush-warm
whisper-kiss of an itch
that has to be scratched—
or kissed back—
just between your ear and your jaw,
until everything in you becomes the
longing to part

your own lips,
your own sea of reeds.

And when
your heart explodes into
one million phantom dancer spirits,
you let the prophecy pour out.

You tell them you've come
to get your drum back.

Na'arah / Maiden

She, who is fearless,
who walks out of the wilderness
feral-shouldered and unbroken,

who is the luscious and undulating ocean
into which all tributaries flow,

who brazen-blooms firm-petaled
like ruby plumeria,

who is immune,
shielded by the perfumed forcefield:
lure of purring tiaré;
tempt of vespertine brugmansia,

who is a downright rhinestone constellation
in a black-velvet-jungle sky,
a millefleur satin-pink-pocketed
concealment,

who has forget-me-nots
darned into
the lining of her garment
by the celestial seamstress
herself,

who is the very mystery
we are discussing,
and the veil,

Rachel Kann

the leap
and the faith,

who dances
rather than collapses
when words fail her,

who is celebrated
for this decision
by the ancestors,

who is teeming with angels
awaiting her every invocation,
if ever she might make one,

who has a standing
invitation to
climb into
the lap of the infinite,
enumerate her wishes
like grains of sand,
like stars,
like dark matter,
like the embodied
waking-dream-state
of actual creation,

who is the round
and unending melody,
the bottomless font,

who is *sovereign*,
who is *daughter*.

And who—
who, among us—
is unbegotten?

Not one,
not one of us
is not thus loved,
(like a righteous sunrise,)
into existence.

Rachel Kann

Doreshet / Seeker-Woman

Your every step
can't help but grind riots
of inquiry into the dusty dirt,
and still, you are unsure.

Your gift is a talented stamina,
an unrelenting continuing
to hunt down the whisper,
intent on catching the scent
of the Infinite.

This emptiness, this mystery,
this dead-set, this wishing,
this what-is-missing,

this inability to fulfill
a prescribed destiny,

this compulsory humility,
this unexpected blessing,
this best worst thing,

this earth-bound
not-belonging,

this ceaseless

yearning.

Ohevet / Lover-Woman

And who would be healer,
if not her?

Who, if not she who teaches
the open secret
of revealed intimacy?

What miracle cure
can there be
above the return to—
and transcendence of—
one's own body?

What prayer more palliative than,

this is a private conversation
between me
and my physical being
and infinity,

this is my mystery
to begin unraveling,

this is my pleasure to seek,
my love to discover,

my spin to
lean into,

my resistance
to press against,

my angel
to wrestle,

my wholeness,

my holy temple,
my flesh,

my breath to follow,

my presence to be presencing?

Precious qedesha,
devotional witch doctor,
whose worship
takes the form of
ecstatic celestial remedy,

who sings,
come to me,
I hunger beyond longing,

who is every anemone
readied nerve ending,
seventh heartbeat,
embodiment,
merged,
heaven,
sacred
yes

medicine.

Tzovah / Templekeeper-Woman

There are infinite secrets in even
the slightest body of water.

The fluid potential
in formlessness
is limitless.

Notice every reflection,
notice the mirror I wield
faces outward,
know what awaits you
though these gates.

Much magic is effected
under the auspices of vanity,
another radar
I am adept enough
to fly under.

We aren't so different,
with our longing to safe-keep
deepest sweetness.

I chose to be made
doorway,

prayed,
contemplated,
apprenticed,

practiced,
risked,
failed,

wiped debris
from these bloody
and bruised knees,
rose to my feet,
learned,
served,
continued

and continue.

I am the keeper
of the house of secrets,

I am the constant
all-encompassing circle-flow:
no one enters this
ecstatic temple
without my blessing.

Meyaledet / Midwife

How holy to give
your own generative soul
over

to space-holding
for the throes of creation.

How divine to carve out
sweet time for this
devotional
revelation-archeology.

What a dedicated shepherding:
to lead the lonely dreamlamb
through the midnight wetness
of the undulating tunnel,

from the dark cave
of secretive sacrifice
into the bright altar-bath
of broad daylight.

The sacred excavation
of helixed antiquity
and brand-newness,

the exhuming of newborn
remembrancer,
the gentle
brushing away of debris,

Rachel Kann

the unveiling,

the making of your own heart
into a hothouse
where the most frangible flowers
can root,
flourish,
grow.

Mekonenet / Mourning Woman

There is an oceanic
pain-knowing,

a tide
no soul
should ever
be made to
swim against,

a depth
no person should
have to go below,

where no diving bell can spirit,
wherein no veiled escape is available,

where the wailing penetrates;
leaks in compulsive melodies
from behind every curtain's
intended modesty.

The Gddss herself
can't help but be
boggled
at the thought
of all that staggering loss,
the roiling sea
in need
of grieving.

There is an edge,
beyond which,
it is enough
to do nothing,
except let
the bends
crack your chest,

relent into the bottomless vessel
life has forged,

all the salt
and water
poured,

expand
past every shore.

Ba'alat Ov / Shamaness

It's not only that
you will be asked to
face your greatest fear,

be rent and completely shattered;
and—notwithstanding—your pulse
will keep hurtling slap-gallop in your veins,

or the demand that you
transcend that battle,
rise resilient enough to
mine your very soul's
alchemized grief,

with no guarantee,
only the possibility
of any extractible medicine—

it's that then—
then, you will become
your own greatest fear,
your own *rather-die-than.*

Swim 18 knots past humble,
36 strokes through humility,
72 drownkicks in humiliation.

The aquatic silence of *bitul.*

The ancestors want to wash
away your trauma
with their own beloved
but badly-battered hands.

The angels hunker,
ready to wrestle,

the demons wait open-
armed for your embrace.

The dead want to whisper
an incessant stream of *what-ifs*
to your waiting listening.

Every magnolia has secrets to sing to you.
Each cedar, a richness beyond riches to deliver.
Obsidian wants to weigh upon your palm.
The whale and hummingbird and lioness, chanting.
The stars are Khima-Pleiading
streams of glow in your direction.

The liminal will not be told how to exist.
The realms do not await our bumbling instruction.
Our plaintive cries for fairness fall
on an unlistening that is galactic.

There are great gifts in darkness.
The light can be injurious, most blisteringly.

I have said more than enough.

Leitzanit / Sacred Fool-Woman

The thing to know is
you know nothing.

Only from this precipice
can you dive into mystery,
be mind-blown,
knocked back in awe.

The humility
to willingly confess,
cop to your cluelessness,
is the sole way to receive
the transmission of wisdom
waiting in sweet anticipation
to reach you.

To be generous enough
to offer yourself up
on the altar,

to sacrifice restrained propriety
in the name of relief,
disarm,

to bring a body to slackening,

to ring the clarion
angel-bell
of a belly-laugh,

this is the most nectar-laden path
a devoted soul can journey,

the sweetest calling
one can answer.

Gevirah / Queen

The crown adorns
she who keeps going,
long enough
for the path to wend
and get treacherous,
eventually;
to the inevitable:
to the crossroads.

The crown adorns
she who will willingly
release this princessly chrysalis,
slip out of her dynastic mantle,
follow the starprints
of naked sovereignty,
choose the narrow bridge
of the regnant.

The crown adorns
she who, with every step onward,
causes consort-baubles
and dowager-trinkets
to tumble, like so much
detritus, toward the bottomless
shard-canyon graveyard below.

The crown adorns
she, who—unshrinking—
breaks herself against
initiation.

Rachel Kann

How could any
bloodborne inheritance,
manmade ordination,
patted approval,

bestow the oleander tree
her own majestic blossoming?

Confer obsidian
her distinct and regal glow?

Grant the magnificent moon
her icy and noble halo?

Eim / Mother

One last contraction,
push.

Flood back into Asiyah Gashmi,
undeniable as the fast-rising sea,
weep for each Rachel and Sara,
every Yocheved, Rivkah and Leah.

Bear witness to their histories' trajectories;
their disappearance from
between the sofer's lettering,
and when.

Let righteous tears stream unfettered,
wetness tracing the web of
inextricable interconnectedness
that zigzags in fantastical switchbacks,
circumnavigating our famously forgiving
heart of a planet.

You are more than womb,
more than nurturance,
more than breast,
more than sustenance,
more than context.

You are earth, sky,
and all that resides in between,

blood, fire and breath,
aleph, shin, mem,

elemental,
manna from heaven,

the mysterious depths,
shefa,

the generous permission of tzimtzum,
no less than a miraculous act.

One last contraction,
push.

Oreget / Weaver-Woman

First, you must feel
the weight of the world.

For a moment, allow yourself
to atlas under the crush of
the heavy weft of regret
nosing above and below
the strained warp
of heartbreak,
over and under,
over and over.

Before the tunnel of midnight
swallows your vision
and the tangle of grief
and wrongdoing ensnares you in
the clotted crush of one hundred
indissoluble thief-knots,

let the venom-nectar
of tarantula medicine spread
on your tongue,
receive this bitterly-needed
sweetness,

picture holy sisters
crocheting a Great Barrier Reef,
imagine a web of gracious creation
woven from utter destruction,

the way fiber
must be scraped against fiber
until they surrender
to the threshing.

Listen to the snap and rip,
let it whisper into winding.

This is the ravel of possibility,
golden thread spun and coiled
in potential.

This is the beginning
of everything.

Chachamah / Wise Woman

She says,
Let me die a thousand deaths,
if only for the privilege
of beginning again.

She understands the
ungloved grip,
the electric twinge
of impossible nostalgia,
that longing to get off-planet.

She says,
There is nothing wrong with this longing;
nothing wrong with your yearning,
nothing wrong with you,

there is no weakness in your grief,
not one iota of brokenness
in your inability to roll with this
regular regimen of sucker punches
life offers up in shameful abundance.

She urges you to
feel yourself,

to resist
falling in line
with hazardous
prevailing paradigms.

Rachel Kann

She says,
Despite popular opinion,
your discomfort
is actually the likeliest sign
of your alignment.

Your lack of resonance
with that which oppresses
the intuitive
is what will save
the whisper within you.

Your guts have always known
the rhythm.

There is no misstep
in your glory choreography.

Your unwillingness
to dance around the issue
will make for the greatest
of entrances.

One more step forward.
The gate will swing open.
Deep breath now,
lean close,

welcome in.

Other Poems for Queens

Mermaid Esther (An Astonishing Fire)

Hold on there, Mermaid Esther,
don't forget: your skillset
has been custom-built.

Remember what you were born for.
You've got this.
I promise that this discontent
is divine, despite the pain
you're swimming in.

Although you're going under,
sister, there will be no drowning today.
Dive unfathomable fathoms deeper.

Rather than look for loopholes,
fashion a life raft
from the strands
of your very real suffering.

Do not be deceived,
this misery
is no doled-out punishment
from on high,

it is a knock at the door
of your heart from inside.

Your soul is an imprisoned star
fishing for clemency.
Let the cage swing.
Throw it open.

You are built of double helixes,
a swirling evolutionary journey.

This life is a spiraling tidepool.
The view of glorious sunlight will
spin round to the dark side of the moon,
as it is bound to do
with every revolution.

I call on you to remember you,
back before you became
your own wet metaphor.

The innocent kid
who turned cartwheels
naked, shameless and pure.

That wild girl who walked
into the ocean,
delighting in the cold bite.

The dreamer who believed
in infinity's limitless possibility.

The precocious princess
not yet stripped of her intuition.

Remember when you
could clearly see the truth
of what was muddying the grownups
all around you?

Rachel Kann

How you'd watch them rationalize,
tell themselves lies,
overcomplicate, bury their pain,
only to inevitably explode later
in the most inappropriate, unrelated,
and dangerous of ways—
over and over again?

Remember the self-sworn oath?
Your vow to never let that be you?
There's no roundabout route to salvation,
the only way out is through.

Don't confuse husk with vessel,
lest you self-immolate.
Subsumed in ocean,
while an astonishing fire blazes within.
You must spill forth this light,
or be consumed from inside.

This is the sacred act
of spark extraction.

This is returning to
the knowing in your bones.

No more ignoring
your internal warning system.
No more denying
inner guidance.

No more collapsing
under the depth charge of confusion.

Sister Mermaid Esther,
gather all of the flooding love
that spilled in surging waves
from every single heartbreak.

Return it to the heart-home
of your ribs,
interstitial glow
flowing out from within.

Toward the shore,
there is a lighthouse
of a little girl,
sturdy-legged,
faithful and patient,

beaming rhythm-encoded
messages to you:

Swim up to the glimmering surface.
Break through.

Our Mother in Exile (For Rachel Imeinu)

While in exile,
she takes it—
at best—to the chest,
waits for redemption,
has no option
but to display a patience
beyond imagination,

is beggar-starved,
told to count herself fortunate
when crumbs of excess
tumble from the table.

Forced into tricksterdom,
she shapeshifts,
hides in plain sight,
sits upon
hidden idols,

learns to swim with the fishes,
or drown trying.
She moves so slowly,
it's as if she is frozen,

entombed en route
to Efrat,
haunting Malchut,
a city built only of words.

Once emancipated
by four-cupped freedom,
she will still need
the sweetening
of everything.

With no struggle,
there is no structure.
With no boundary,
there can be no holding,

only light, a spilling
unchecked.

She wrestles
with the best of them,

presses
the vessel
into existence,
a thing forged
for receiving,
stretched, even,
fashioned for expansion.

Meanwhile,
Infinity
wants nothing so much
as to fit its limitless rampant
vastness
into the littlest of spaces;

to be contained
in her very
dazzle-garden.

Rachel Kann

The Deborah Number (Shirat Devorah)

This Devorah-heart is a
four-chambered thudding,
a coven of buzzing and judgement,
of song and prophecy.

Find her buried beneath the palm tree.
Break ground in the rooted moonlight.
Knock upon the locked entrance.
Rattle that exhumed cage.
Sing her into awakening.

Even the stars have been enlisted
in this celestial battle.

How little brotherly
love can one holy sister subsist on?

This is the question
she does not want to respond to,
despite this, her very existence
is its own expansive answer.

She is a contiguous bee-melody
that dance-hovers divination
above hyssop and eucalyptus.

She whispers,
Nothing is fixed.

With enough patience,
even mountains of limestone
melt into the sea
in the face of unsayable greatness
and infinite divinity.

It's physics.

Everything flows like honey,
eventually.

How the Garden got Started (Eve Speaks)

Let me teach you a secret.
Read the blank space.
Learn the art of seeing emptiness
as intimately as lettering:

With beginnings, (   ) created **Gd.**

Behold the lush unfolding,
all of existence
pregnant with my potential
from before the beginning—
with which I was created.

This is how the garden got started.

It's not that we didn't have bodies,
it's that they were not consequential.

Understand that all of this:
this gathering of atoms
is made up of more empty space
than solidity.

This is how the garden got started.

There is no time before me.
(This is the futility of hiding from
that which you are made of.)
I did listen to the serpent.
I did fill myself with pomegranate.

My thirst is boundless.
My devotion is total.

Etz Chayim,
winding spirals, eternal helixing.
Branches and blossoms,
roots and trunk,
earth and sun,
the abundant generous love-flood
of without-end/ever-becoming.

This is how the garden got started.

Rachel Kann

Other Poems

את

If this word is made fresh,
then let every alleged blemish be blessed,
each individually kissed
like the exquisite mezuzah it is.

There is a doorway
that all of creation
thresholds its way through
on its way to
the eternal-unfolding-already-was.

Oh, All-That-Is/Infinite,
who whispered this lintel
into existence,
into becoming,

who bears witness
to this living-thing-ness,

who is this lintel,

who is the whisper,
who made the making,
who forms letters out of breath,

who said,
Let this את
contain the whole expanse of it,
the vessel and exhalation.

This is the breath,
this is the mystery,
this one, right here,

this is the Saturn-moon-ring
that surrounds everything,

the embrace of beginning
by ending,

the way the wax
makes love to the wane,

this:
this is the faithfulness
you are held with.

The Higgs Field: Each Green Unfurling

Can you imagine the practical grace
in your thoroughgoing pulsation?
The surge of blood toward and from,
the electric whisper of your heart's continuing?

Do you grasp the implication
of your lungs' twinned genius?
The expansion and contraction
in eternal pranic tango
with each green unfurling?

The gift of
paroxysms of laughter?

The wonder
that is your stumbling journey?

The elaborate code
of your elegant animal?

The miraculous machinery
of your is-ness,
if you could witness it,
would knock you to your knees in awe,
raise you to your toes in grateful praise

to the greatness that set the tempo,
made momentum out
of the ineffable substance
our every atom is pushing through.

The Gift

Don't I know this
feeling of homelessness,

and don't I know
how real the loneliness
in your bones is.

Slow down and notice
the gloriousness afforded;
the view through the newly-opened window
of your broken heart.

This gift of clear vision.

Think on
the sacred company
you're in:

has there been one instance
of wisdom
in the history
of this misbegotten existence
elicited from anything but heart-brokenness?

It is an act of generosity
to shatter the packaging,
to peel the encasement,

to reveal your true soul's face and,
say, with outstretched arms,
Here, here is the shape of my heart.

There is nothing left
but to be swept
away by love.

Exile and Redemption

If it seems like everything's shattering,
that's because it is.
We've arrived at this
particular moment of crisis
precisely to be
called to our highest.

This struggle
is our undoing

and this uncovering
is breaking forth

the awakening of our spiritual ancestors
and successors,
extending endlessly in both directions,
our supernal lineage gathered
through collective intention.

To hold is to conceal, yet
we are meant
to create vessels
that enable
incremental revelation.

Imagine Eden, ablaze,
spilling with radiance,
no space for revelation—

Rachel Kann

how to hold a candle
against a backdrop of
infinite spilling light?

We are built of mud and dust and blood and water,
of lust, thunder, questions and wonder, of
internal fertile-walled whispers.

Exile and redemption:
separated
by barely a breath.

All of this Outrageous Beauty

Even in the very act of contraction,
you long to be expansive.

It feels like
life is trying to drown you,
choke you out,
like life is a formidable opponent,
like shaking your foundation,
like breaking you open,
like *holy holy holy.*

Step into the meadow.
Listen to the sycamore
creak in heavy wind,
breathe.

Think on the bravery of the seed:
it cracks open
without even knowing
what it will one day be.

This merciful universe
keeps delivering opportunities
to dig in the dirt,
to work.

Creation is built of desire.
If you experience longing as discomfort,
hunger as suffering,
how will you be able to create?

Rachel Kann

What will you do
with all of this outrageous beauty?

The Truth of Love

Love is a force,
stronger than
you've ever given it credit for.
It is not the passive submission you fear it to be.

Love is where the rubber hits the road.
Your suffering does not make you a stranger,
it makes you human.
Discomfort is guidance from your soul-compass
toward what really matters.

The out-of-tune piano prays to be played
in new ways,
refuses to be discarded,
wants its good parts to be made useful,
longs for new melodies
created from the invention bred of necessity.

Awakened,
we can no longer afford the luxury of unconsciousness,
its price now outside our purview.

Praise be to these united states of broken hearts,
these shattered instruments of transmission
forcing us to see with new eyes,
to feel with raw-nerved belief,
to fly with no net,
to go collectively off-script,
to dismantle the illusion,
and know the truth
of love.

Rachel Kann

We Could Be Dancing

We all have a heartbeat,
rhythm inborn,
which means
we could be dancing.

Everything in the material world
is under the spell of its respective shell.

We traverse the darkness.
We'd rather be shattering
the packaging,
despite the fact that we're scared,
because light resides in there.

This universe
was/is/will be
spoken into existence.

The open moan,
alchemized into meaning
by the bite of words,
restricted by lips, tongue, teeth:
outpouring and restraint.

We are masters of expansion and contraction—
we all breathe.

Before the jail cell was ever built,
first came the key.

If we could see our celestial cheering section,
we would know the meaning of liberation,
we would know our souls' success
could not be called into question,
we would know our true nature is vibratory.
We couldn't hold back from dancing.

Illumined Nation/The Rededication of Space

When the world is upside down,
I/Me/Us/We must flip the script:

grab hold of the narrative,
revolt against the same old story,
resist the riptide of history
despite grim odds,

the plot twist brought
to untwist this plot.

Thus begins every
inner rebellion.

I/Me/Us/We enter
the cold wetness
of the cave
made of echo-stone

to retrieve the oil
hidden in secret
and maccabean
shadow-folds
for generations.

When the world is upside down,
I/Me/Us/We must flip the script:

Watch the exalted letters
dance into all possible combinations,
account for every permutation,
precisely as numerous
as each luminous star
in the numinous field
of our milky and honeyed galaxy.

I/Me/Us/We reclaim our sovereignty
over the landscape
of our heavenly body,
shore up our borders,
draw constellations as boundaries,

rededicate the sacred space
in the center of us,

sanctify the nourishment
of moon and sun.

Let us rise elemental,
offer our/self as vessel,

four mothers to the left,
four angels to the right,

we long to be anointed, filled with
hyssop and frankincense,
spikenard and myrrh,
balsam and cassia,
jasmine and rose,
holy olive.

Rachel Kann

Pour in the gloaming
moment of every tiny brave blaze
thrown in stark relief

against the gift
of mysterious darkness.

Haneshama Lakh

I/Me/Us/We
am/are
all for you.
This spilling starlight of soul?
yours.
This spiraling miracle of infinite mechanisms?
You built it,
fashioned a fleshly starship
out of husks of crumbling galaxy.
I have evidence:

your fingerprints are all over me.
My body is a prayer.
My body is a pleading.
My praise, a relentless pulsating.

Our heaviness bows the branches of your tree.
All drinking of the same circulating.
Have mercy.

Here is my humanity:
I am flawed.
Awkward and broken,
ripped seams
leak gleaming moonbeams,
there is nothing else for me but to wholly give over.
I lean into you,
bend to you.

This leaning is my leaping.
Let me unfold into your embrace.
Let me let you hold me.

The sweetness of your gracious interceding:
I am creature,
crafted to be as I am.
I am open to receive.
Let me take you into me.

Despite the heavy velvet bloodcrush
of our earthly transgressions,
part the curtain.

Teach us to forgive ourselves
for missing the mark.
Let us learn from your gentleness.

Show us how to love.

Stumbling
through paradise,
hypnotized by flash and numbed to true substance,
derailed by the chanciest circumstance,
distracted by the weakest of cheap glitter.

We are putty in your hands.

We are drowning in our own failings,
rationalizations, miscalculations,
and outright transgressions.

Dissolve all separation, let us
come together like the ocean we are:
droplets indivisible from one another.

I/Me/Us/We
am/are
all for you.
This spilling starlight of soul?
Yours.
This spiraling miracle of infinite mechanisms?
You built it,
our heaviness bows the branches of your tree.
All drinking of the same circulating.
Have mercy.

Purify.
Rectify.
Ready.
Mercy.

Rachamim.

Pasturing Amongst Roses: A Prayer for Elul

"I am my beloved's, and my beloved is mine,
who pastures among the roses:"
—Shlomo HaMelech, *Shir HaShirim*

Let I/Me/Us/We begin
with begging forgiveness
for this petition's penitent repetition,

my/our mission is driven
by persistent and specific wishes
we are incapable of dismissing.

I/Me/Us/We are the opening,
the ten-thousandth gate-swing,

I/Me/Us/We plead
for clemency,
to be sprung from this linguistic prison.
Decolonize my/our verbal volition.

Repair the damage
of landlocking
my/our oceanic tongue,
mermaid-mouths choking on ashes,
sand, shell-shards and beach glass
crammed down our collective throat
by those who would silence this
life-giving defiance.

I/Me/Us/We long to know that this
abject loneliness
and shattered brokenness
will come
to untold wholeness,
heretofore-unknown seventh-leveled
pleasure and respite,
sweet completion,
a deep knowing that I/Me/Us/We
am/are supposed to be,
am/are meant for present existence.

Disabuse I/Me/Us/We of the notion
that we don't belong here.

Let us be healed from this
terminal and toxic
soul-sickness
brought on by unwantedness.

I/Me/Us/We are pasturing amongst roses:
let my/our devotion be known,
we subsist on only blossoms:

consume just blooms,
fill our hungriness
with bee-buzzed budding,

drink of sweetness,
quench our thirst on
thirteen-petaled mercy

Rachel Kann

make us worthy of learning,
may we be deserving of awakening,
may our faith be greatly warranted,
may we receive our invitation
to the garden, and

above and below,
body and soul,
let our every petal unfold,
let our every sense open,
let us know the generousness
of wild, abiding and unbounded
love.

Dogwood Winter

Between you and me,
(and the blooms
and the trees,)

even the breeze
who incessantly sweet-talks the rose
knows she was born thorned
for good reason.

I admire your resistance,
your unwillingness to give in
to overwinter,

how you take truthful root
in the loam, deep-weave
beneath the earth's surface,

how you flush with heat-blossoms
out-of-season, a profusion of flowering,
a beautiful refusal,

how you face off
with cold snap,
spray unending petals
from calyx
in blatant rebellion.

Rachel Kann

Consider Jacob,
who knows enough
to be terrified
at the sight of all those angels,

knows it means
there is need
for guarding.

In the Time of our Sorrow

My tongue wants to un-gate the flood, it is
an urgent compulsion to spill knotted guts,

in these weeks of banned melody,
my lips want to rebel,
to howl,
to sing

of my suffering,
of all my shortcomings,
every rejection,
every threat to our collective existence,
the abandonment unabated,

of how my heart is a bitter almond,
spilling with cyanide,
splitting its endocarp,
longing only for the orchard,

of how my heart is a heavy stone,
flak-jacketed,
sallow and sinking in my chest,
how a glut of shrapnel is stuck in my throat,

of how I am blindfolded in love's minefield,
frozen, unable to navigate the danger
lurking beneath the surface,
hurtful blossoms
lying in night-wait
only to explode,
detonate the light of day,

Rachel Kann

of the world's unending
re-dedication to the re-destruction
of temples.

My heart wants to take flight,
transcend the gravity
of this misbegotten planet.

Before the unkindness of ravens and
murder of crows can escape the open moan,

I am circle-dancing,
hand in hand
with Magda and Miriam,
who came through the dark tunnel of the Shoah,
who are here with me,
present and spilling light.

We weave a grapevine
up the trunk of the almond tree,

this world crushes,
refuse to turn poisonous,
dancing and rooting and branching
despite this.

In glorious defiance,
we pour ourselves forward
in honeyed amaretto flooding,

we sweeten the darkness,
light the bitterness.

We kasher every unholy implement
used against us.
We ready them for service
in the holy temple of our most
miraculous dance:

our continued existence.

The Big Bang

I
The Big Bang is not a thing that once happened.
The big is still banging,
not just reverberating,
but actually in the act of currently creating.

II
If you're anything like me,
you know how it is to smell pine
in the crisp sunlight
of morning and feel like a stranger,
you're banging against the edges of this world,
trying to find your place.
You're less interested in the rules of man
than the mind of the divine.

If you're anything like me,
you are suffused with a love
that cannot be hidden,
a radiant pulsating rhythm.
You want nothing more than
to lie side by side in the sun-warmed sand
in a pool
of foolish
midnight moonlight
and

talk about how the infinite exists within the finite,
about how a soul could be cracked open by ecstatic math,
how a soul could be cracked open by awe,
a soul could be cracked open.

Loving Thunderously

Loving thunderously like you do,
there are times when your heart
continuing to beat
has to be enough,

when there is no soft landing,
and all the options seem wrong,
every road, a dead end.

When you find yourself
in these dire straits, and your breath
perpetuating its clockwork rise-and-fall in your chest
is the day's greatest accomplishment,

celebrate
the stubbornness of that second hand rhythm,
your resistance of the urge to rip wheel from cog,
stop short the whole operation.

Loving thunderously like you do—
like ten thousand galloping hooves,
like playing chicken with infinity,
like biting into that apple,
like abject dedication,
like an adept,
like every
door
of every
house of worship
flung open to the influx of sunlight—

there are times when it feels like dying,
bent over backwards
under sackcloth and ashes,
the warp and weft
pressing into your pliant flesh.

You are built of outstretched
arms, each spilling
with Damascus Roses.

In the depths of your most exquisite loneliness,
know this:

in The Grand Call-And-Response
with All-That-Is/Infinite
that makes up the substance
of our earthly existence,
you are the melody
resolving.

Dancing Lesson, or How to Let the Words Leave You

V
For once,
this is easier done
than said.

But only because
it is unsayable, unnamable,
beyond language's latitude,
outside word's jurisdiction.

Allow this.

VI
Collect all of your suffering,
all of the discomfort in your own skin,
the belligerent self-criticism,
pain and frustration,
righteous resistance to inequity,
your distrust of self and others,
every nagging memory.

Do not muck around in it,
the trick is simple acknowledgement.

Then,
offer it up.

Rachel Kann

Hollowed out, now
breathe, now
there is room for the sound to infuse you,
rhythm resonating through
the earth,
soles of your feet.

VII
Remember when you were
very small?

In a very big room,
you were consumed by the music.
Spinning and jumping.

You let loose,
you were overtaken,

your face,
in abject blissful expression.

Then you felt it happening,
panicked.
You separated from the moment,
and sidestepped into observation.
You shut down the sensation,

swallowed the smile whole.

This is the part
when your mind wants to fight you.

I promise it is worth the struggle.

I've yet
to have anyone regret
passing through this gate.
Shame is a stubborn lock.
Pick it anyway.
The combination is inconsequential
where we are headed.

Kick in the door if you must.
Bust.

Turn away from your reflection,
expectation,
your projections.

Know the glory of your physical instrument,
the infinite wisdom,
the shock absorption of hinges, cord,
the way your hips want to unfold in
golden meaning,
how your arms want to spread
and your sternum wants to lead
and your head wants to throw
back.

Know your sweetness,
your purity,
your innocence,

know this is more than permitted.

Rachel Kann

VIII
All that is left:

ineffable.

Mooncode

Forgive me,
I'm a simple human woman,
built of sinew and blood.

Is it any fault of mine
that a million moonsongs
have already been sung?
Make this a million and one.

I escape the stifle of industry,
step onto the black-topped parking lot.
Small wonder,
I am knocked out by that
glamorous pearled vamp
of a luscious moon,

consumed by her luminous profusion,
drowning in her riotous lily light,
weak-kneed and wholly devoted.

My foolish lunatic heart longs
to present her to you,
a diamond sphere on a silver platter,
to compare your glow
with her heroic waxing fantastic.

Born fat-souled
as we were,
we relate to her
unabated craving to radiate,
to fill center stage
of a star-charged sky.

We cannot be flattened,
our only diminishment,
an illusion of eclipsing.

Amidst this celestial silence,
I will speak to you only
in mooncode,
intricacies of rhythm
wherein my enfolded heartbeat is hidden.

If this missive
is successfully transmitted,
bridges the distance,
all of this will have been worth it.

When we wane,
our light retreats,
closed,
hearts
dulled by
disappointment.

But when we are full—
Love—
when we are full,
the honey of our illumination runs
riot.
Thunderous,
glorious,
superrational,
unbidden,
explosive.

Our brilliance is in our resilience:

We always come around.

What to Tell the Children

Tell them that this is the great awakening.

Tell them that we humans
have made some huge mistakes
and that's how we now
find ourselves in this tenuous place.

Teach them that hate is the poison.
Teach them that love is the remedy,
that it is better to be readied for what comes next,
even if the revelation is painful.

Tell them that this is the paradigm shift,
that the old is collapsing in on itself,
that this death rattle is simply a temper tantrum;
the last gasp of a dying goliath.

Remind them of how they get wild
when they are most tired,
and then pass out,
that this is what it's about,

That this is what is happening
to a decrepit and ineffective empire.
Tell them that everything is not ok
and knowing that is ok.

Tell them that pretending
that what is unacceptable is fine
is what got us to this

sick and dysfunctional spot
on the timeline.

Apologize for any prior attempts
to teach them denial.

Tell them you were blinded by desire
for comfortable numbness.
Express that you had the best of intentions,
that you were working within a broken system,
where few benefitted at the expense of many,
that you laid low,
kept to the status quo,
obediently played your role,
but those days are over, because
now you know better.

Tell them that they have no responsibility
to follow someone blindly
based solely on a title.

Teach them to practice discernment.
Tell them authority and respect
must be earned and are not inherently deserved.

Teach them that there are
good people
from every background,
ethnicity and belief system,
that they must align themselves with kindness,
that there is no more time for divisiveness.

Rachel Kann

You tell them
that just because something is legal,
that doesn't mean it's right.

You tell them
to stand up and fight.
Remind them of all the lawful atrocities
committed in the twisted history
of this violent country:

That Rosa Parks righteously broke a law
and the world took notice,
that Harriet Tubman
is our modern-day Moses,

that women would not be allowed to vote,
and no one would have proposed another notion
if the blessed rebels hadn't taken a stand.

Tell them love will win this war,
but only if we remember
that love is not just one unending cuddle puddle,
but fierce as a mother bear protecting her cubs.

Tell them that although this existence
is damaged beyond repair,
they must not despair,
there is possibility,
and we will willingly
and willfully open ourselves
to new ways of being because
the old way is not working,
has never worked,

and the world deserves better,
and we're worth it.

Tell them they are not free
while another suffers
under enslavement.

Teach them that we are all limbs
on one body
and we cannot chop off our own arm
without deep suffering.

Teach them humility,
but also to re-learn to trust their intuition
and beg their forgiveness
for unintentionally misleading them previously.

Tell them their gifts are useful.
Tell them they are beautiful.
Tell them they are the truth.

Other Queens

In Service to the Queen

This life is
a shaky construction,
made of
brief punctuations
of sweetness in an
endless run-on sentence
of ache.

There is no guarantee
that the journey
will be worth the grief
in the final summary.

There is only
the knowing
that no matter your struggle,
there are hundreds
of someones
who would give it all up
just to trade their trouble
for yours,

that no matter how sturdy
the foundation,
every castle crumbles
to dust
in the end,

that no matter how dynastic
the blood,
we are all made
into beggars
eventually—

knocked to our knees
in the face of
awe almighty,

that we have no ultimate control;
that no matter the planning
and precautions taken,
unspeakable terror awaits us.

There is only
the longing,

the ghost-trace
of the taste
of honey
on our remembering
tongues,

the way we pray
like so many ladies-in-waiting
for its sugared return,

the unending buzz-hope of
our homeless bumble-dance
from jasmine blossom
to lavender bud.

Rachel Kann

This hunger
is what is meant
to keep
our hearts beating

until our sentence is complete,
all our time served,

until we are liberated from this
prison-hive,

having sacrificed everything
in service to the queen.

Tu B'Av Bullerengue

"…Y si el dueño pregunta, hay la verdolaga
Dile que yo te mande, hay la verdolaga"
—Sonia Bazanta Vides, "La Verdolaga"

We daughters of Shiloh
waltz into the vineyard
clad in borrowed garments
built of brilliant blue-white
stardust and time,
purified in the ways
of the ancients,
plunged in the ritual bath.

We are rebuilding with each twirl,
we dissolve separation,
we bless each vine
with prayers of abundance,
each step presses grapes
to transmutation,
claret splash-stains spreading
against our lily dresses.

We seven sisters
dig our own graves,
sleep in them for as many days,
awaken each morning
under the blazing desert sun,
until we finally
dance out of them
into full moonlight.

We priestesses
guard the stars' secrets,
usher our days of mourning
into our moment of celebration,

praise what frays,
wrap wick-lengths
around the graves
of our ancestors,
dip them
in soul-candles
of beeswax.
This is the breaking of the ax,
this is the end of destruction:

Know that
this restoration existed
before the shattering
ever began.

Burn This

Medusa hides behind my eyes,
fears her own reflection,
wants to wend her
way inward.

I refuse
passage to
leatherblack asps who
attempt escape by virtue
of spilling from my lips.

I swallow them
back rather than
birth them into
material existence.

Twinned sirens writhe
inside my ribs,
mean to seduce,
chant tunes
intended to consume me
within the fluidity of grief.

I claw my way up
through this wet-broke and
broken aloneness.

In direct spite of
naysaying and detraction,
my pulse still runs amok,
the maddening thudsmash
stays unstuck in defiance
of those who desire
no less than my
anesthetized quietude.

The mermaid who swims
in the center of me
remembers
two words
uttered shamanic in
marosa-response:
don't drown.

The sorcerer's apprentice
under my skin
wanders in the grit
of city-midnight,
the air, eerily still,
the moment,
stiff and thick
with inexhaustible possibility.

The moon is a milky pitcher
pouring pearlescence
down;
my crown.

Empty threats,
simple resistance,
rejection,
damage,
abandonment,
estrangement,
danger,
they are not enough
to stop me.

I was built
resilient,
made to withstand
much greater than
petty distraction.

I am elemental-celestial,
fashioned by the
hands of my ancestors
from their very own
prayers and bones.

First, palo santo smoke,
then, the commingled aromas
of hyssop and rose,
next, the rhythm of drums,

and after that, comes
the wet mystery
we've whispered of
for millennia.
This is viscera:
blood and gutsy.

I was forged
in the fiery furnace.
It takes way more
than enflamed war
to
burn
this.

Another Star/Another Queen

As the spiral of time unwinds and
we reach the inner tightness,

as the tension increases and
the spin speeds up to meet this,

what we experience
is the physics
of the quickening.

From within this simultaneously
terrifying and sacred chaos,
I emanate.

I know my sovereignty.
Let history belittle me,
label me disobedient,
I place this designation
as a jewel in my crown.

I'm not one to listen in
to the pitiful whimper
of egotism,
thus missing
the whisper of divinity.

This is my resistance,
my defiance,
my refused compliance.

Rachel Kann

Know this:
there are definite limits
to what the laws of man can accomplish.

They can demand my degradation,
murder me,
make a monster of me,
but they are powerless
to legislate my soul's autonomy.

The secret to freedom
is realizing there is no approval to seek
from within an infrastructure
that is—at best—complicit in your utter destruction.

My crime?
unwillingness to be paraded around
in my crown,
unwillingness to be a trophy,
a puppet,
a pawn.

My crime?
I'd rather be having my own ingathering
than awaiting an engraved invitation
to objectification.

My crime?
Honoring my majesty.

Sisters, we are in the midst of
massive metamorphosis.

Transformation, by nature, is
inherently treacherous,
but this does not permit us
to remain in stasis.

Before this dissolution could even begin,
our imaginal cells were whispered
into new manifestations of existence,
nascent potential awakened.

We are the budding of new wings.
We are the opening.
We are the infinite unfolding.
We are bravely entering the space of not-knowing.

We have faith in
what awaits us
in the liminal spaces
beyond the reach of
intellectual limitations.

We are reawakening
in the garden,
in the season of our sweetness,
completing our receiving,
in a state of love so deep,
we soar
in awe.

Rachel Kann

Rock the Bells

You ring the bells,
we are the bells you are ringing.

We plant the seeds and
you are the blossoming.

We are the sweet relief
of direct communication.

We are traveling
via vibrant vibration.

We tendril down from heaven,
celestial made manifest.

We transmute our nature from supernal
to elemental,

unfurl
earthly form
to bridge the connection.

You ring the bells,
invoke the listening.

We are radiant,
burn hydrogen to helium,
translate astral
into bloomed brugmansia.

We are the bells,
flooded with light,
brilliant beyond gold,

so bright,
we are achromatized.
We emanate gleam-strands
of luminosity,

antennaed
eight-directioned,
seven-sistered,
sixth-sensed,
fifth-dimensioned,
four-lettered,
three-starred,
two-flamed,
oneness.

The ringing is the gathering.
The ringing is the calling.
The ringing is the song you are singing,
the song you have been listening
for eternally.

New Style Inauguration

In an endless desert
outside of time,
a circle of priestesses
practices augury:

they watch the skies
in a state of ancient ritual divination
enacted in cases of
religious, business, and political
decision-making for millennia,
interpreting birds' flight patterns
as guidance in crucial matters.

They are known as augurs,
and they are currently
watching in horror.

Note the sturdy word-trees
the augur's birds perch in.
Their roots go deceptively deep.

It's worth disturbing the peace
and digging in the dirt
to get to the genesis.

Inauguration:
a ceremony
wherein birds' actions are observed
by augurs practicing augury.
a political decision would be made

and a leader would be
inaugurated
based on the ways of the birds,

which is why I've been
viewing hawks circling,
noticing crows sweeping in,
beholding hummingbirds honeysuckling,

I'm seeing bald eagles
tendering their letters of resignation,
unwilling to be guilty by association.

I've been breathing in natural secrets,
studying the bumblebees' choreography,
burying my nose in blossoming floripondio,

laying hands upon all manner of
rock, crystal and mineral,
listening to the whisper of wind and river.

This is the gist:
The wisdom arisen from competition
and ego assertion is worthless.

It's high time for a new-style inauguration.
Time to repo hijacked linguistics,
get really specific,
and get down to business.

This is our ordination.
By the power vested in we,
by our collective soul-agency,

we hereby declare
we do solemnly care.

We care about love
so much,
we will endeavor to
bask in full moonlight
as often as possible,
to dance,
to hug,
to laugh,
to feel awe.

We do solemnly care enough
not to go radio silent.
Not to choose blindness.
Not to keep quiet.

We do solemnly care
for the plight of our sisters and brothers.
We know that if we're not speaking up,
we're not even in the galaxy
of doing enough.

Safety-pin sentiments are lovely,
but they won't pierce the veil
the way it needs to be
to expose
the horrific inequality
and actually change what
we must no longer tolerate.

This tricky society will
gift us for our complicity, it
deeply desires our silence.

We do solemnly care enough to
rise up and
defy this.

We do solemnly care about this quickening,
we are listening.

We do solemnly care,
even though
exposing our hearts
does make us easy targets.

Regardless,
we lay down our weapons,
we drop our defenses,
these walls are so senseless.

We do solemnly care
enough to be hopeful.

Best be on our best behavior.
Best maintain our integrity.
Best step up to our greatness,
we know that it awaits us.

Best believe
the high priestesses
will be watching the skies,
auguring
closely.

Rachel Kann

The Beginning

If you can find stillness,
the jasmine will night-bloom in your direction,
and the breeze
will carry its sacred exhalation of perfume
toward you.

Breathe,
the moon will cascade waves of radiance
downward,
drop her silver robes,
glow.

You will awaken,
overtaken by a love from within
that asks no permission,

golden particles rising
beneath your skin.

All of existence
longs to be an offering.
Eternity is a constant whisper
wishing to be listened to.

This is the beginning.
This is only the beginning.
Let it in.

About the Author

Rachel Kann is a poet, performer, ceremonialist and teaching artist. She's a 2019 WORD: Bruce Geller Memorial Prize recipient. Her poetry collections include *A Prayer on Behalf of the Broken Heart* and *10 for Everything*. She is the author of the children's book, *You Sparkle Inside*.

Her writing appears in journals such as *Tiferet, Eclipse, Permafrost, Coe Review, Sou'wester, GW Review* and *Quiddity*. She's a resident writer for *Hevria*, where she's also featured as a performing artist on *The Hevria Sessions*.

She's performed her poetry in venues such as Disney Concert Hall, Royce Hall, The Broad Stage and The San Francisco Palace of Fine Arts.

She is a 2019 Inquiry Fellow through American Jewish University's Institute for Jewish Creativity and was a 2017 Asylum Arts Reciprocity Fellow and the 2017 Outstanding Instructor of the Year at UCLA Extension Writers' Program.

Her Spoken Word Visual Album, *The Quickening*, has received accolades from film festivals in Florence, Tel Aviv, Los Angeles and New York.

She leads Realize Paradise Soul Journeys and is initiated as Tzovah through Kohenet: The Hebrew Priestess Training Program.

This book was written with the support of WORD: Bruce Geller Memorial Prize. WORD is a program of American Jewish University's Institute for Jewish Creativity. WORD: Bruce Geller Memorial Prize is made possible by the late Jeanette Geller in memory of her husband Bruce.

The Jewish Poetry Project

Ben Yehuda Press

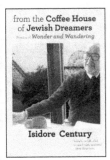

From the Coffee House of Jewish Dreamers: Poems of Wonder and Wandering and the Weekly Torah Portion by Isidore Century

"Isidore Century is a wonderful poet. His poems are funny, deeply observed, without pretension." – *The Jewish Week*

The House at the Center of the World: Poetic Midrash on Sacred Space by Abe Mezrich

"Direct and accessible, Mezrich's midrashic poems often tease profound meaning out of his chosen Torah texts. These poems remind us that our Creator is forgiving, that the spiritual and physical can inform one another, and that the supernatural can be carried into the everyday."
—Yehoshua November, author of *God's Optimism*

we who desire: Poems and Torah riffs by Sue Swartz

"Sue Swartz does magnificent acrobatics with the Torah. She takes the English that's become staid and boring, and adds something that's new and strange and exciting. These are poems that leave a taste in your mouth, and you walk away from them thinking, what did I just read? Oh, yeah. It's the Bible."
—Matthue Roth, author, *Yom Kippur A Go-Go*

Open My Lips: Prayers and Poems
by Rachel Barenblat

"Barenblat's God is a personal God—one who lets her cry on His shoulder, and who rocks her like a colicky baby. These poems bridge the gap between the ineffable and the human. This collection will bring comfort to those with a religion of their own, as well as those seeking a relationship with some kind of higher power."
—Satya Robyn, author, *The Most Beautiful Thing*

Words for Blessing the World: Poems in Hebrew and English by Herbert J. Levine

"These writings express a profoundly earth-based theology in a language that is clear and comprehensible. These are works to study and learn from."
—Rodger Kamenetz, author, *The Jew in the Lotus*

Shiva Moon: Poems by Maxine Silverman

"The poems, deeply felt, are spare, spoken in a quiet but compelling voice, as if we were listening in to her inner life. This book is a precious record of the transformation saying Kaddish can bring. It deserves to be read. These are works to study and learn from."
—Howard Schwartz, author, *The Library of Dreams*

is: heretical Jewish blessings and poems by Yaakov Moshe (Jay Michaelson)

"Finally, Torah that speaks to and through the lives we are actually living: expanding the tent of holiness to embrace what has been cast out, elevating what has been kept down, advancing what has been held back, reveling in questions, revealing contradictions."
—Eden Pearlstein, aka eprhyme

Texts to the Holy: Poems
by Rachel Barenblat

"These poems are remarkable, radiating a love of God that is full bodied, innocent, raw, pulsating, hot, drunk. I can hardly fathom their faith but am grateful for the vistas they open. I will sit with them, and invite you to do the same."
—Merle Feld, author of A Spiritual Life.

The Sabbath Bee: Love Songs to Shabbat
by Wilhelmina Gottschalk

"Torah, say our sages, has seventy faces. As these prose poems reveal, so too does Shabbat. Here we meet Shabbat as familiar housemate, as the child whose presence transforms a family, as a spreading tree, as an annoying friend who insists on being celebrated, as a woman, as a man, as a bee, as the ocean."
—Rachel Barenblat, author, The Velveteen Rabbi's Haggadah

All the Holes Line Up: Poems and Translations
by Zackary Sholem Berger

"Spare and precise, Berger's poems gaze unflinchingly at—but also celebrate—human imperfection in its many forms. And what a delight that Berger also includes in this collection a handful of his resonant translations of some of the great Yiddish poets." —Yehoshua November, author of God's Optimism and Two World Exist

How to Bless the New Moon: The Priestess Paths Cycle and Other Poems for Queens
by Rachel Kann

"To read Rachel Kann's poems is to be confronted with the possibility that you, too, are prophet and beloved, touched by forces far beyond your mundane knowing. So, dear reader, enter into the 'perfumed forcefield' of these words—they are healing and transformative."
—Rabbi Jill Hammer, co-author of The Hebrew Priestess

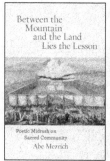

CPSIA information can be obtained
at www.ICGtesting.com
Printed in the USA
BVHW031055171221
624293BV00002B/185